THE HEARING HEART

Leonard Clark

The Hearing Heart

London · Enitharmon Press · 1974

First published in 1974 by the
Enitharmon Press, 22 Huntingdon Road,
East Finchley London N2 9DU

© Leonard Clark 1974

SBN 901111 47 3 (cloth)
SBN 901111 48 1 (wrappers)

Limited to 500 copies

*Printed in Great Britain
by Daedalus Press, Stoke Ferry, Norfolk*

CONTENTS

EYES AND VOICES

Eyes watching.
                    I see them now
searching me out in this half-light murmur
where evening's stars put small windows in dark trees;
a surveillance of glances, lonely and questioning,
moves along soft-breathing borders,
calling me to sleep
and young lovers in avenues under
parallels of cool limes, humming with heavy bees.
The eyes are unwavering.
                    I do not flinch from their gaze.
Let them be blind to the ugly visions of present time.
They peer from dead skulls,
witnesses of yesterday
I remember in the sunlight,
pince-nez with lorngnette, fichus and spidered veils.
They are all watching.

And voices.
                    I hear them now
speaking to me in this half-heard silence
where morning's sun prints first shadows on diamond lawns;
a sprinkle of words, lively and loving,
falls through drowsed summer air,
calling me from sleep
and hidden birds in woods beyond
lines of old fields, green-bladed with new corn.
The voices are insistent.
                    I cannot escape from their echoes.
Let them be silent to the harsh babel of present time.
They sound from dead lips,
whisperers of yesterday
I remember in the shadows,
panama with cartwheel, blazers and silk blouses.
They are all speaking.

And voices have eyes,
eyes, voices.

GRASS

'What is grass?' the child asked,
and Whitman gave a poet's answer,
explaining nothing. Dürer
painted a clump of it,
formal and brilliant in German air.

I ask the same question now,
looking out on winter pastureland,
but can only find a rational answer,
am more ignorant than the child.

Blake would have interpreted it for me,
Samuel Palmer, ecstatic and dazzled at Shoreham.

And yet I know grass almost by heart,
its touch, colour and rare scent,
common, yet strangely individual,
beautiful and everlasting, since
first I rolled down childhood hills,
my body smelling of summer,
the strong life entering me.

And how many times have I heard them chime,
the belled quaking grasses, in soft wind,
a delicate peal for unencumbered days,
or walked, a green and wondering man,
through small forests of cocksfoot, foxtail,
red darnel, brown bents and brome,
sniffed sweet vernal in old hayfields,
the mowers moving westward with the sun,
held a broad blade of couch grass
between stiff thumbs, blown a sharp note
over river banks, scattering dragonflies,
threaded stems with wild strawberries,
spattering their blood all the way home.

Barley and oat shall cover me at the end,
my dust become panicks and fescues.

Rain falls, the grasses silently grow,
larks hide their pearled songs in dark growth,
alien with sorrel and chamomile,
pimpernel holds up its poor man's weather glass,
a lost village is buried deep, flint and coin,
a king's bones blanch beneath matted roots,
cattle and cannon tracks photographed on turf.

Grass is my security,
my firm hold on time,
that takes me, hour by hour,
from flying husk and seed
to brittle flakes at my dark end.
I never see a solitary tuft
lodged with the frost in pavement cracks,
but feel its hidden power
to burst from the prison holes,
suddenly swell, break the stone,
cover the ruined world again
with huge, primeval fields,
savannah, prairie and steppe,
running from the mountain to the sea,
shining and undefiled.

I sense the potency of that tuft in me.

CHILDREN IN TIME

O, my son, my daughter, born
Late in time, but perfect, whole,
Steered in by prayer (winds threatened to wreck),
Balanced on hope now,
You inherit Time's gifts, under your palms
The four seasons wait; sea, stars,
Folded within your bones, you live, grow complete.
Sit down and sing with me,
My children, rock the world to sleep, rock.
Now take this bread and eat, this meat,
Bread and meat of joy.

I see a face in the dish, and old tears,
Stiflled by Time's ease;
This was my son, too, this
Was that other, born
Winds and tides ago, nay, half-born,
Out of time, and maimed.
I watched the flowers fade in his starved cheeks,
Sound, trickle like sawdust from his lips;
Death plundered him, in time, the grey shadows
Covered him with silence.
The seed was mine, corruptible.
Come, child, from your formlessness,
My hand is here (Like as a Father),
Sit down and weep with me;
Then take this bread, this meat,
Eat sorrow's meat and bread,
For they are thine, and mine.
My children, sorrow and joy are Time's companions,
O, my daughter, my sons.

REDBREAST

I was mistaken.
Tricked by time, thought you heaven's bird,
The little crowned lord of winter,
Because with bleeding bill
You plucked out thorns from that doomed head
On Calvary's hill;
I heard your unexpected note,
Honoured your appearances.

Now I fear you,
Fallen angel of my sky,
Prologue of misfortune.
Evidence of time's revenge, you seek me out,
Harrow me in black seasons.
More terrible than the albatross.

You came with no compassion
The day first love broke;
You watched its autumn funeral.
A second time, looking through
A summer window,
Where a baby drew small breaths to death.

Now I am at peace with time,
But, malignant bird, blood is on your head,
You crucify me still with song.

THE OLD KING

'And so the old King died – '
The voice whispering the tale
Stopped on a sigh, when a bird suddenly called
Over far, fringeing trees,
Secretly, surprisingly, a curfew there;
Sang on and on, snatches of sharp song,
Punctuating the windy dusk
With half-remembered histories.
We listened, ears cocked to the recollection of dead wars,
Burned out now, dusty with skeletons.
It was a song of triumphs won, flags furled,
Gentleness under the sun, intense, beautiful.
It was a song of apricots ripening on hot walls,
A painted barge riding kingcups and weed,
Velvet children with nervous hands, wet-lashed eyes,
A bow twanging.
And then, tomorrow on its knees, day done,
The bird flew away with the song.
' – and was buried with music.'

FIRST POSTING

Looking back now as through a flurry of snow,
details blurred though not the remembrance,
there were those villages in Devon I knew
at my first posting, houses
sunning themselves in combes, moors
bleak and barren, except at lambing time, beaches,
sanded half-moons glinting at low tide;
hedgerow banks tumbling with primroses
all the crazy way to Kingsbridge, 'God,'
said the schoolmaster at Modbury,
'God at His most vulgar.' Everything green and wild
beyond Black Torrington, Zeal Monachorum,
the moon dipping low into the trees at Cornwood,
Ugborough's church tower in rain.
O, those villages with the thatched names
chime in my head, a peal of marriage bells,
Ipplepen, Germansweek, Sticklepath, Prawle,
Berry Pomeroy, Holne.
And always children in high-windowed schools,
the warm country vowels on their slow tongues,
trudging in from red farms, through gates, faces
glowing from all weathers, reading books so worn
they had their grandparents' finger marks upon them.
Yes, those were the villages.
But Plymouth, too, burning, burning, nights, days,
everywhere terror, skies scorched with flame,
my own heart's house falling in ruins,
I smell the burning still, I carry the scars
still, I hear the sirens still, my head
is full of mourning, a peal of funeral bells.
I had better remember the villages, the names,
the children happy, and singing,
the old songs of the corn harvests, the tales
of long-ago smocked summers,
and dabbling in the dew.

CHILDREN OF ISLINGTON

They creep out of shabby houses in long back-streets,
Inhabit a kingdom of desolate places,
The day's wild fury continually throbs and beats,
Night's fever written deep on pinched-up faces.

They seem to have passed beyond the world's loving care,
As if childhood itself suddenly had stopped,
Their innocence doomed, wilting away in the public glare,
And over each a cage of misery has dropped.

They know too much of sadness, vulnerable and young,
Will not all come to a season of full flower,
Nor shall a spontaneous song lie rejoicing on every tongue,
To flood the firmament with a vision of power.

There is small comfort here for these castaways, where
Sour rooms breed resignation behind cracked panes,
A babel of quarrelling voices bludgeons the frenzied air,
And grief goes dumb and sullen whenever the sky rains.

And yet upon their drooping heads a little sunlight falls,
Whose beams are stronger far than laws and politics,
And when across the roofs a bird at morning calls,
There is a glory on the black and crumbling bricks.

They dawdle back at evening to the clamour of the slums,
That greed and gracelessness have long contrived;
What hand can turn these festering wastes to new Elysiums,
And not a single child neglected and deprived?

THE DAY HARDY DIED

The day Hardy died,
January, early on in the year,
I was at home, in Gloucestershire.
Fields stiff with frost,
Trees in splints, the dangling sun,
Crucified;
No bird
Fluttered the dead air.

He was 88, I, not free of boyhood's fire,
Waited my Pentecost;
He had written his last, spare word,
I, at my spring, had scarce begun.

I did not hear the news
Until evening, when I sat alone in the inglenook;
I had walked to the inn beneath bright stars,
Past gravestones, churchyard yews,
An empty sheepfold.
My eyes drowned in a book,
I did not see the man who slipped in out of the cold,
But heard him say to one of the regulars,
'Thomas Hardy's dead.'
Nothing more was said,
Nobody seemed to care
Thomas Hardy was dead.

I began to think of the Mellstock choir,
Remembered a drawing of a very old man sitting upright,
Folded hands in a grandfather chair,
Said to myself the lines about oxen in a byre
Kneeling at midnight;
The death itself had small significance.

But now, many winters away
From the chill circumstance of that day,
Ground still hard, every bough

Birdless, bare,
I cannot believe it was just chance
I was there
Sitting in the inglenook the day Hardy died;
For he has been my winter guide,
And only a moment in time separates us now.

DE LA MARE'S BELL

This was de la Mare's bell,
Brass, reflecting what it imaged,
Minute, distorted, upside down,
The handle, a black minaret on its tower,
Its tiny tongue,
Time's clapper, tinkling like glass inside.

It used to rest on the table by his bed,
With flowers, a clock, and books
Unopened or half read.
I often saw him lift it gently up,
The old fingers twining round the wood,
Then shake it into dulcimer sound,
Very kind and pleasant to the ear,
Its voice chiming clearly through the Twickenham house;
A few charmed seconds, and then
The bell was brought to dumbness, the air was still,
The Roman head sank back to rest;
It was all over.

And I used to think how like de la Mare his bell was,
Fragile, haunting, sure, precise,
Sounding boards for dream and the indefinable.
And now, de la Mare dead, the flowers dead,
The clock counting out life elsewhere,
My son rings the bell,
Rings it, not for a poet's passing or curfew for night,
Rings it, innocent bellman, through childhood's frail house,
Through twilight, moonlight, the soft shades,
Listening forests of stars,
The dusty pavilions of Time.
But, O, if I rang till doomsday's crack
I could not bring him back.
Let this blithe bellman ring.

S.T.C.

*(Died Highgate, 25th July 1834: Re-interred St Michael's
Church, Highgate, 6th June 1961)*

Limbs twitching, head in stars, see him come
Bravely from Gillman's house in the Grove, this man,
This visionary, saddened by tears and opium,
In whose veins the sacred river ran.

He treads once more the haven of the Highgate air,
Peers weakly at life through guilty eyes,
Entreating his tongue to mumble some prayer,
Taste again the holy milk of Paradise.

The air is suddenly on fire, old dead stir
To jog along with him, to share his loss,
This poet, dwindled to mad philosopher,
Jilted by fate, slain by the albatross.

There was death in the fingers of that young one's hand,
Another, mercifully drowned, made romantic farewell;
Nothing worked out for him as was planned,
Susquehanna, a dream, the dome of Xanadu fell.

And now, in a new time, his drugged visions gone,
He drags his poor bones to their final place,
This genius, Coleridge, whose naked spirit shone
White-hot with angels, and saw them, face to face.

THE PEA-PICKERS

Travelling north, a glazed afternoon in June,
the train slowed down, and stopped. Lincolnshire,
and men and women picking peas in flat, hot fields.
I watched them in their bended silence, a few minutes or so,
moving forward in ragged lines from row to row,
beneath a huge, unbroken sky. Pea-pickers.

They wore the same grave faces as their ancestors,
prisoners of the land, who worked these meadows
all weathers, fingers in frost, rain whipping bowed backs,
from turnip-hoeing to barley-time,
bonnetted grandmothers, babies humped in hedges,
long-pinafored, with wooden dolls from Peterborough Fair.

The signal dropped. We started up again.
They did not notice it, continued following the sun,
locked in the solitude of timelessness.
I thought of Clare, soaked through with dew,
picking with them, first light to sundown,
poems in his wild eyes, lonely for love;
and Cobbett, caustic and critical, riding these fields,
stuffing his head with figures and facts.

But most of the great cycle of the years,
morning at seed-time, starlight at harvest,
peas planted, butterfly flowers, tangles of tendrils,
pods swelling, haulm withering to death.

And if, by chance, this time next year,
I should come this way,
these old acres would be new again with peas,
pickers still dumb and stooping there,
patiently moving forward, baskets crammed,
the self-same rhythm, season after season,
life, death, and resurrection.

LODERS

A land of old hills beneath wide skies,
A crazed pattern of fields, pasture and corn,
high hedges overhanging lanes of campion and hartstongue,
trees dotted over the speckled landscape, and farms
tucked in hollows, flotillas of clouds;
a land out of time, solemn with silent witnesses.

The sun eases away the last drops of dew,
cows move with their shadows out of steaming milking sheds,
a flock of gulls dips in from the sea,
settle as one bird along stubbled lines,
a tractor puffs away the morning,
crisp barley gathered in;
a man strides with dog and gun across the slopes.

A vision of innocence, fresh as rainwater,
childhood returned again with warm, dead voices;
Samuel Palmer saw it at Shoreham in stooklight,
Wordsworth among his lakes, Thoreau in hickory woods,
Clare's poems dropped with his sweat on holy turf;
Beethoven heard it in bird-song, his ears unstopped,
Michaelangelo, upsidedown in the Sistine Chapel.

I breathe some of its divinity now,
am washed by it as these hills are washed,
know that Love is shining here, everlasting;
give back what quickens my heart,
kindles my dulled eyes;
and have a taste of harvest honey on my tongue.

IN NORFOLK

At the back of the primeval marsh,
stockades of reed and rush, river-green,
smooth cornfields flow in tawny tides
up and down the landscape, out of sight.
Wafered butterflies float the untroubled air,
a pheasant treads out of the straw shade,
jewelled and arrogant into the sun's firm eye;
it is a sacramental afternoon.
And I have come to my safe lodging here
in the hallowed light of harvest,
as if all Knapton's angels were flying over me,
these fields flaming with cherubim;
I am one with Breughel's immortal reapers,
praying their sickled way to evening,
I stand redeemed in golden meadows,
Blake's New Jerusalem.

I pluck a single ear of corn,
feel its strong divinity,
a barley-needle draws my blood,
and I am lifted up.

COUNTRY CHURCH

Pigeon and daw nest in the flint, bats
drop their foulness from wormed roof,
dust settles on psalter, merchant's monument,
there are cracks in the north aisle windows,
the seven-sacrament font silently crumbles,
smell of decay in the air.

Brass rubbers come on summer afternoons,
take away black image of knight and lady,
say no prayers where once the Host was lifted up
above the painted loft, pews were packed
with squire's silk family, servants from the Hall.
A congregation now of watching eyes
sees the dozen or so who slip out of the winter dark,
and, believing, kneel at the altar rail,
to wait a few more quiet years
for old graves to be re-opened, names and dates,
carved upon family stone.

Museum or church? Ruin or shrine?
It does not matter which.
The building stands, alone, shadowed by great-boled trees,
tower seen for miles across open fields,
witness still of worship and prayer.
In time, the chancel arch will be repaired,
the grasses cut, the sanctus bell ring out again,
the office said by other lonely priests;
and over the lichened wall,
new seed be sown,
new harvests reaped and gathered in,
and all the Company of Heaven praising there.

HILLS

have names, shadows,
farms tilted in the green folds,
rain driving sheep along thin tracks
into mists that lose themselves near the sky.
Hills have curlews crying, heather
rolling purple tides with singing bees
over and over, up, down;
thyme drugging summer's small air.
Snow lingers in crevices, hides all wounds
an extra month or more, winter streams
tumble with loud voices into valleys,
there are trees carved by the wind.

Hills should not be ploughed, let grass
rule them with rock and solitude,
the dead sleep on in their long barrows;
let hills be, rabbit and hawk
fight out time together.

HEDGEHOG

Comes out by day in autumn,
exploring hedgehog, betrays himself
snoring loudly in leafy ditch;
plump with summer's fat, moves along,
battering slow way through dry twigs.
I hear him lumbering, hairy head appears,
then all his ten-inch prickly length,
makes for the bank, senses me there,
rolls into a ball, waits for the attack.
I leave him alone though, curled up on the hill's lip,
this earth-brown savage, enemy of frogs.
He'll chew beetles and mice to powder, hear
every small noise in undergrowth,
will take on snakes by the tail,
bayonet them with needle-spines.
Shy of the sun, dislikes company,
cannot see far, a fine swimmer,
drinks milk.

BEES

I

Bees do not follow fashion,
subscribe to earth's laws,
are ignorant of man's whims.

This morning's bees behaved golden,
like those that honeyed Samson's lion,
made Olympus wildly hum, swarmed
in Shakespeare's garden, saw Cortez
marching grimly through Mexican forests.

This evening's bees murmured when Rome fell,
whispered a victory song in Charlemagne's ear,
moved forward in clouds with Genghis Khan,
ravaging the steppes, lulled smocked villagers,
dozing in hay fields at seeded summer.

Bees live the minutes for themselves,
servants of their own wax empires,
trespassers and secret travellers.

II

You can hear them softly at first light,
foraging unseen in clover fields.
You can see them plundering the late limes,
when all else is dream, slow shadows.
You can smell bees each smoky harvest,
loaded and dipping towards packed hives.
You can touch them, curled up and motionless,
suddenly chilled by the frost.

MOLE

Curled up in leafy fortress, secure,
I am the little black lord of the underworld,
proud and solitary in my tight plush;
prince of the sappers I have excavated the whole of Europe,
hills and tunnels advertising me all the way to Japan.
My four strong ounces drive forward at speed,
long, whiskered snout ramming the stones and roots,
leaving the damp, night-tubes behind,
sun and wind unfriendly aliens
as I lift up earth into the cruel light,
clawing out worms and grubs, gorging myself.

I do not see well but can sniff out stoats,
hear lightest footsteps hunting overhead,
will fight to the death with needle teeth,
once killed a sour king;
am not interested in my naked young.

Winter come, I go down deeper
into my freezing element; do not sleep.
No fool, I am fearful of farmers, cunning traps,
the indignity of transfixion on bush and wire.

I am a strange character,
persistent and quarrelsome;
you would miss me though if I disappeared for ever
with dodo and dinosaur.

Better leave me alone to my dark moods.

GROUND ELDER

For nearly a week that open-aired autumn
we worked, slowly digging the pestilence out,
spades slicing the heavy soil, sun and rain,
fingers sore, and clawing at the matted root-stocks,
cursing the small veins creeping all ways like paralysis.
Ground Elder. I hate the coarse and greedy plant.
Nothing to look at, it has neither mercy nor modesty,
insignificant flowers, seeds in league with the wind,
'growing of it selfe without setting or sowing,
fruitful in its increase', as Gerard wrote in anger,
watching the vile herb stealing his Holborn garden,
garrotting and smothering all other vegetation.

Yet the weed has virtues,
or thought the old monks who planted it,
innocently in their cider orchards to cure the gout,
or fed apple-glutted pigs to keep them from sudden death.
They called it Bishopweed, out of reverence;
and Culpeper would have you eat its young leaves for paleness.

Truth or herbal nonsense? Enemy or friend?
I, who fought it for five broken-nailed days,
found no answer, but condemned its persistence,
preferring all my joints to ache, even the fiery gout,
to those endless furrows of cruel Ground Elder.

A cunning deceiver, its white impudence will come again
with next summer's cuckoos.

POEM FOR CHRISTMAS

At the flowering of the thorn,
Snow in valley, ice on hill,
Christ, the eternal rose, is born
When all else is winter still.

Oxen bend adoring knees
In each dim and midnight byre,
Every eye there clearly sees
Rafters ringed with holy fire.

Winds are hushed for some small space,
Not a breaking wave moves on,
Trees are locked in one embrace,
Love renewed, all chaos gone.

Silence, and the heaving earth,
Wrapped in Eden's innocence,
Waits enraptured for the birth
And the smell of frankincense.

Darkness trembles with new light
From a single, dazzling star,
Prints a stable on the night,
Bethlehem in the calendar.

Creatures that were stricken dumb,
Find at last a human voice,
Know what mystery is to come,
And in unison rejoice.

Quiet now, the Child is here,
See what beauty floods the air,
Greater than the nails and spear,
Or the crown that He must wear.

At the flowering of the thorn,
Snow in valley, ice on hill,
Christ, the eternal rose, is born
When all else is winter still.

THE COIN

A ten peso piece. Gold,
thin as faded leaf,
1535, head of Holy Emperor.

The museum swam away through tears,
anger boiled in my veins.
I did not see the resurrected coin,
small and solitary in its glass case there,
but the great and embracing sun, god of all life,
rayed out in glory,
celestial, at Atahualpa's back,
burning the heart out of the scorched land,
rock fortress and rainbow cascade,
the naked terraces at Machu Picchu,
moon-temple hung with silver.

And Pizzaro, treacherous and blinking gold,
waiting ruthless at Cajamarca, blood
in his sheath, the Virgin on his breath,
spilling doom and disaster
in the name of Christ, the Inca,
restless by the hot springs, collar of emeralds,
blazing at the setting of his sun,
feeling the dark omens softening his bones.

And then, murdering the stillness of the cool room,
the sound of lying voices at the fake trial,
fires crackling, flames leaping higher,
the proud captive led out by drums and torchlight
to the stake at sundown, Pizzaro's false tears.

Betrayed and strangled, a common criminal,
this coin, the Inca's frail memorial,
if it could weep its last pale gold away,
its tears would flood the square at Cuzco,
drown all Peru with grief.

LEARNING BY HEART

At least give me some hope
When I come to my end, you
I tried eager enough living to learn
Thoroughly by heart, which is by love,
Will not go back from me then, turn
To me still with some word.
You gave what you could
(I hold the ashes from that wood)
When I, burning in love's heat,
Dry of spirit, needed more
To land me safely on your shore.
Snow frilling the curtains of northern air,
I came a beggar at your door,
Cuthbert in my bones, mumbling a prayer,
I said my fiery cross of words then,
Cannot say them again;
You know them well.
What the meaning, purpose of all this?
Is it something past praying for?
I think it needs the dolour of a passing bell.
Or if the whole matter be true,
It is for me to be flooded over with your tide,
Drowned in you,
See Death buried with a kiss.
Fulfilled, there to abide
(Master, there is yet one word to read)
Some praising particle with Bede,
Having at last when I come to depart,
Learned by heart.

PLAINS

In a star-deserted hour,
Light and snow are equal with pain,
Winter finds comfort in dead power,
Love marries the dark to live again.

Not to think, not to feel,
Not to hope for a second birth,
Is for death to break in and steal
The Eden fruits of earth.

Clouds cover the face of the sun
When friend beds down with enemy;
Midnight and dawn are one
In heart's neutrality.

LETTER FROM ROME

By the waters of Rome I sat down.
                              And wept.
Wept when I remembered.   You.

The first time, carried you with me
in memory's eye, as if you were there,
live as the sun.
All Rome an island, thought we were exiles,
consenting to a brief pact,
watching the fountains, domes in the blue morning,
exploring each other at sundown.
Many times felt for your hand.
                              It was not there.
I took my grief to the Palatine.
                              None to comfort me.
Knew what real sorrow was then,
I, his blood companion.

A second time I walk by Tiber,
you for ever out of my days,
silent, distant, and comfortable.
Thought I saw you yesterday in the Forum
under the arch of Severus, cool as history,
golden and classic.
                    It was not you.
A man put his arm around her shoulders;
They strolled on into the afternoon.

Again in the Borghese, a woman by a tree,
I believed was you.
                    Her children ran to her.
I turned away into the shadows,
became more stone than any statue there.
Prayed in a dozen churches at belled evening,
found tears where the Host burned,
alien voices, the worn steps.

And somewhere behind red curtains,

a violin playing a Siciliana;
I could not bear its melancholy.

A girl, lithe and beautiful,
spoke to me in a dark piazza,
gave me her hand, her loneliness.
I fled from her, hot and trembling,
not wishing to betray you,
mingle my anguish with hers.

You have unsexed me, not knowing it.
Perhaps it was ill-starred and foolish,
this bond I had with you;
I knew it could come to no flowering.
Yet have no envy for any other,
nor can any other for me.
                    Who have nothing.

Do not pity.
          I do not require it.
Continue to wonder that love can go on,
not wither away by these sad waters,
joy, too, my right hand has gained in cunning,
can write to you from a strange land.

And do you have tears?
I think they may fall sometimes for me,
alone, anonymous, where leaves fall,
the bruised marble bleeds.

There will not be a third time.
I have turned this city into a place for the dead,
the lost and abandoned ones.
Only the dry grains of my love remain,
waiting for some cold resurrection
whose shapes I do not know,
but from which may curiously grow,
before last darkness closes in,
a few fond blades of pale grass.

[37]

THE COPSE

After the strong climb into the morning sky,
they left the track for the dewed fields,
turned downhill, gulls wheeling above,
over a criss-cross pattern of tractor ruts,
and came to the copse.
She shared the small secret with him,
his head already planted with childhood trees.
Two score of autumns returned for him again,
with beech leaves lying in crinkled layers,
blackberry tangles, rose hips burning,
silver birds on mossed branches.
She moved through the soft stillness,
gathering bracken for the year's ripe festival.
Her arms filled with huge harvest fronds,
the copse became love's crucible,
she more golden than barley meadows
or sun westering in full radiancy,
he an Inca priest at his glad worshipping.
A new element suddenly discovered there,
the heart's alchemy proven.

LIGHT RECOVERED

The long wood, balanced on the hill's lip
beneath a sky, dun as a trout's back,
sees the weather defeated by arum's new sheaths,
and daisies dotted over sodden meadows.
The wood is littered, needles and cones,
heads of pines block out what light there is.
Walking without words along snaking tracks,
they search for some relevation,
a gospel for the heart.
There is none but spring's green face on buds,
no movement of resurrection;
blinded by winter's cold neutrality,
they have forgotten what light there once was,
how it encircled them.

And then at the tunnel's end,
a single ray breaks through, suddenly,
marrying the meadows to the rising hill,
piercing with laser beam the tangle of undergrowth,
embracing them, as they embrace,
light recovered.

FEAR NO MORE

He has hanged himself in the glebe,
this man, who loved, and was loved.
It could not be.

      First light, sheep are standing stones in dew,
      backs to the breeze, fleeces curled with gold;
      mists move with ghosts along the hills,
      a mole is at work in the graveyard.

She sleeps on in the silent house,
eyes swimming in young dream;
morning has not touched her yet.

      Rooks are calling death in mouldering elms.
      see from their tottering pinnacles
      the taut body swinging in dumb air,
      slowing down to the wind's last breath.

They did not choose this way,
seek to be castaways of time;
came gently to their destiny.

      The stream's cold water is ruffled up;
      he will not hear the clock strike its execution hours
      over the heads of grasses, daisies
      opening to dawn's first flushing.

It could not be.
There was no freedom for them,
their years did not marry.

      And now the fields tremble with small sounds,
      every stone is baptized with grief,
      a far cock betrays the night's ending,
      a living man is walking the slopes.

She is awake now,
will be brought soon to her breaking;
their child knocks for release.

He dangles in space, out of time,
dumb and blind to the world's censuring;
his shadow printed on the wet turf,
has become the sun's stiff finger.

CHANGES

He came into the breathing dark
to calm his wild heart's ranges;
ashamed of showing tears he left
the ringers at their changes.

The owls were calling up the night
with mists along the valleys,
his eyes were drowned but still could see
the rise and fall of sallies.

Caught by the moon the paper moths
around the tower were fluttering,
nor did they seem to hear, nor care,
what doom the bells were uttering.

And she stayed silent ringing there
beyond his hope of taking,
but knew what agony for him
that surge of sound was making.

A load of grief upon his back
he stared at graves and wondered
why time was flying with the wind,
if all their days were sundered.

He chose the spot where he should lie,
the sombre bells still swinging,
and knew that soon upon this ground
her children would be ringing.

The lights go out, the tower is hushed,
and silence dews the meadows,
she looks for him with eyes of love
and draws him from the shadows.

UNDER EGGARDON

Iron man, speak to me
from your litter of bone and shard,
where now on summer turf I lie alone,
brooding, perplexed,
beneath your graveyard hill,
breathing this valley's unbearable silence.
Speak to me of the frosted days,
the starved tribe huddled together for warmth,
fearful under dumb stars,
horses whinneying in the long dark,
snow levelling the maze of ditches and banks.
Speak,
you who lolled away
the summer minutes in thyme-scented grass,
scabious trembling, cattle
shadowing the carved slopes,
skylarks singing over water and wood below.
How was it with you then?
What unseen terrors clutched at your throat
each fevered night among embers and sling stones,
waiting for the god at morning to shine?
Speak, furred man,
I have no comfort here,
millenials of grief away from you,
no answers to any questions I ask myself
before my tears turn to iron.

> Living man, I do not understand,
> and did not ever know.
> I felt only the wind's blade,
> the wild assault of the rain on my skull,
> and saw the brooch I made for her,
> fading in cold hand,
> my eyes remembering.
> I met each labyrinthine day as it came,
> went to my lonely end.

I took what I could while it was,
gave back what was given me,
held in my tears.
Living man, live,
love on.

FALLOW

The light is Dutch light, clear, serene;
the old masters knew it, Ruisdael and Avercamp,
Vermeer at Delft, January afternoons,
spring at sleep in their palette-boxes,
frost hung fresh on muted grass,
vermilion sun folding up over black dykes,
as now it picks out this one field,
flooding it for an hour or so with ochre.
A few hungry birds peck at nothing,
skeleton hedges have short shadows,
a broken harrow rusts away time.

The field is fallow,
lines clean, and waiting,
life working silently beneath the turf;
on either side, plumed kale, viridian,
new furrows, dark as umber.

And lovers, too, have their seasons of fallowness,
when fires are low, yet still are glowing there,
a time to rest, mellow and silent;
waiting secure, in winter's sunlight,
another seeding, a fuller harvest.

The old masters knew it.